Bi

Beaks and Bills

by Linda Cernak

illustrated by Kristin Sorra

Harcourt

Orlando Boston Dallas Chicago San Diego

Visit *The Learning Site!*

www.harcourtschool.com

When you go out your door,
you can see birds roaming
everywhere. What a show!

Birds use their bills to help them get food. Each bird has its own kind of bill. A bird bill is also called a *beak*.

Some birds eat seeds. This bird has a short, strong bill. It helps the bird crack the seeds.

Some birds eat bugs. This bird looks for food near a road. It uses its bill to eat bugs that hide.

This bird has a sharp bill.
It's good for eating bugs in
tree bark.

Some birds eat plants. This bird has a long, flat bill. It helps the bird eat plants that float.

Some birds eat fish. This bird has a long, pointed bill. It is just right for catching fish!

This bird eats fruit. Its yellow bill is very long. The bird uses its bill to grab fruit from tree branches.

This little bird sips nectar from flowers. Its long, thin bill fits right into the flower.

This bird made her nest. Now she gives the baby birds food so they will grow. Who would think birds use their beaks in so many ways?

These people give the birds oats and bits of toast from bowls. Be kind to the birds you see. They are our friends.